4TH AND A LONGSHOT

My Quest to Become the First Black Punter in the NFL

NATHAN SCOTT

BlesScott Company, LLC

4TH AND A LONGSHOT

4th And a Longshot is a work of nonfiction. It is based on actual events and facts. It includes accounts of real people and details of real places, organizations, and events; however, names and characters except for the author, Nathan Scott, have been changed. Any similarity to real persons names, living or dead, mentioned is entirely coincidental and not intended by the author, except in the mention of public figures and places.

Details of some sports team organizations have been changed to protect the identities of the persons involved.

ISBN: 9798985687026 (hardcover)
ISBN: 9798985687033 (paperback)
ISBN: 9798985687040 (eBook)

www.4thandalongshot.com

Contents

Prologue: Aspiration

The story of my football career is about, perhaps, the greatest punter who never punted in a National Football League (NFL) game. Though it was a tragic end to what could have been a great career, I still live, with the scars of rejection and the sadness of one terribly bad career-ending decision. It's a true story—names, except for mine, may have been changed, yet the events were not.

The story is also about a career-ending injury that was the result of something rarely discussed in media rooms but mostly in locker rooms to protect the ugliness of the lack of sportsmanship! An ugliness that highlights selfish purpose and a lack of consideration for players' futures, health, and financial well-being. It's an ugliness that's always been part of the game but remains a conversational taboo. The ugliness is called bounty football.

There are literally tens of thousands of young men yearly who aspire to be professional football players in certain positions. Many began their journey at different stages of their lives. They come from all levels of society—the rich, the poor, and the middle class, all having the same dream. Although they're quite different in the roads they take, they face the same two outcomes: success or failure.

Though these two outcomes are diametric opposites, they are fueled by the same factors: skill, favor, finance, effort, and determination, or the lack of any or all. There are also two less considered factors that are just as important and influential. One is the decisions we make at certain points in our lives, and the other is the decisions that other people around us make that can directly affect the outcome of our situations in positive or negative ways.

This story brings all those factors into play, particularly the two less considered factors, which worked together to direct the outcome of one such dreamer who hailed from a difficult place.

A place where young men and women from all cultures dream of escape using sports as an avenue to success.

But many of them are oblivious to the fact that the beginning of their success marks the end of someone else's, because the number of positions available on any football team at any level is limited. So, when one wins a job or position, someone else loses out and is either sidelined or leaves.

Another way to look at the situation is to consider that whoever is trying to get the job is trying to replace someone's friend on the team. A friend who's shared months or even years of struggle in grueling practices and tough games. Teammates who've been through a lot together don't like to see their friends replaced. It is another less-known aspect of the fierce competition on any team.

In American-style football, there are two positions that have seemingly always been screened from Black players: quarterback and kicker. Quarterback, on one hand, was said to be too complicated for Black players, requiring quick thinking and unequaled courage. It was alleged that Black players possessed neither, and over years of controversial tryouts, it was proved to be just a process to disqualify Black candidates. Nevertheless, there have been several, some of whom have reached the pinnacle of the position: Super Bowl quarterback/MVP.

There have only been a few Blacks who pursued placekicking as a full-time position. Most had to have been good at another position to even get a kicking tryout. Although there have been a few who were given the opportunity to kick in the NFL, I'm sure there have been others who were also capable, maybe even better than many who made teams. In most kicking tryouts in which I participated, when a Black kicker missed his second or third kick, it was evident that he wouldn't make it.

The other kicker position is punter, whose job I believe is one of the most important of all the positions on the field. Quarterbacks can throw interceptions and keep their jobs. A placekicker can miss an occasional field goal or extra point and still not worry about his job security.

A punter on the other hand has to be on the mark most of the time. Missing punts or having bad punts can cause the defensive to wear out very quickly in a game. A punter has to know how and when to hit certain types of punts and be able to pull them off when needed. They need to know how to avoid dangerous punt returners or at least how to make it difficult for them to receive a punt.

As with any position on the field, many young Black men aspire to be punters and work hard to get there.

The punter is probably the most important of all the specialty positions because game control can be forfeited by bad punts. The ability to continue to force your opponent to start deep in their own end of the field is a psychological weapon as well as a physical one. It takes strategy, skill, courage, and confidence to pull off different types of punts when needed under a variety of conditions, things that Blacks have been accused of not being able to do.

One negative that will be experienced is that most teams at any level don't have kicking coaches who have actually mastered the art of kicking. My main focus is where I did, and that's punting.

I very strongly would suggest kicking and punting camps where the experts have honed their skills and teach them.

As for punting in general, it must be mastered to be an offensive and defensive weapon. Growing up, I knew nothing of camps and had to learn to master effective punting by accidentally hitting bad punts. That may sound a bit controversial, so let me explain. Whenever I made a bad punt while practicing, I considered why.

The right time to perform the needed result at a given time in kicking a football makes the art and mechanics of punting like a chess game, with the kicker knowing what must be done before stepping on to the field.

The position of kicker—both punters and placekickers—appears to have been screened to favor non-Black players. There were no Blacks who were hired or given player contracts to be punters until the 1970s. As of today, there has been fewer than ten recorded in the history of the NFL.

I was one of the rare Black punters who loved the position and aspired to play in the NFL. This book tells about the efforts I made, the obstacles I overcame, and the unfortunate end to my hopes and dreams. By sharing my story with you, I hope to inspire young Black kickers and foster change at the highest levels of the game.

Chapter 1

The Love Of The Kick

"Hell no, man, it was bounty! They had bounty on you, and you knew it. Me and Shala are going to take you to the hospital. Baby, go get my car."

On the way there, he hit a bump. My knee shifted as I lay in his back seat, and I about crapped my pants. All I could say was, "Where's my Corvette, man?"

"Your buddy Harold said he'll keep it for you."

"Noooo! Not that fool, man!"

Arriving at the hospital, I was seeing images of crabs in a bucket, pulling those trying to escape back into the bottom.

Approximately Twenty Years Earlier

In the late 1950s in a small segregated neighborhood called Eagle Ford, I had been walking about a mile and a half to school since the first grade with other Black children. Every day we passed White children who were also on their way to school as they walked on a hill above the road and threw rocks and other things at us about fifteen to thirty feet below. This caused the

Black kids to run as fast as we could to avoid being hit, though the shouts of racially charged hate hit us every time. The upside to having to run so often was that it allowed many of the Black kids to develop very strong legs.

From this I began to love running, so I made a game of it. I would often challenge other boys to be the first to clear the present dangers of the thrown objects. I would even run when nothing was being thrown our way, both to and from school, challenging myself to run as fast and as far as I could.

Yet weekends presented a very different situation for the boys. Our fathers, who worked side by side in a union-controlled company, were separated by ideas of race in their communities. There was one section called the line, where Blacks and some Hispanics lived on the same street, even next door to one another. There was the white line, where only White people were allowed to live, and there was what we called little Mexico, which was populated primarily by Hispanic families. Though we lived in segregated areas, we often got together on an open field and played football.

I was first introduced to the game of football when I was in the fourth grade. Teams were majority Black or White except for special occasions where there were not enough players of the same color to fill a team, and we chose to mix rather than to not play. I would stand on the sideline and watch, not being old enough to play with the junior high and high school boys. Though I was, for the most part, large enough and strong enough, the Black boys would not allow me to play.

Besides my age, another reason they wouldn't allow me to play on the team was because they knew I had an eye injury. The summer before, there were teens playing with their slingshots, and one guy launched a triangular piece of steel used in making concrete. It hit the corner of an apartment building and ricocheted, hitting me in my left eye and imbedding a chunk of stucco into my pupil.

I tried to tell my parents I was having a problem seeing out of that eye, but they didn't physically see any damage and told me it would get better. Besides, my dad couldn't see a reason to waste money on a doctor's visit, but by the time school started, I could barely see light through that eye and was almost blind in it.

Mother finally convinced him, saying, "This boy can't see out of that eye. We need to get him to the doctor." The doctor referred us to an optometrist, who prescribed glasses that never helped.

The injury altered what could have been a very different life for me. Athletics was a part of my DNA—I had many relatives who played football and basketball, and my father was a very talented baseball player who was also very good at several other sports and positions, including a very good running back in football. In baseball he played shortstop, third base, and outfield, but his favorite was pitching. He played in a Black baseball league as a pitcher and outfielder. In those days if you started a game, you were expected to finish it.

I recall watching Dad pitch in a game where he was doing so well, the whole infield sat on the bases and just watched. Only one hit was allowed, but it was a single shot down the third baseline, which turned into a triple. That was the end of those types of antics.

Dad never warmed to the idea that his son favored football over baseball, and he never knew that the eye injury had lots to do with that decision. It never stopped me from trying, but hand-eye coordination proved to be a major problem for most of my life until I had an operation on that eye in 1988, when I was forty years old.

First Kicking Experience

Back to neighborhood football when I was a little boy. I watched the other kids play until one of those special occasions occurred when the White team did not have enough players and I was asked to fill in.

"Oh, let's just let him kick," the White team said, even though they said I could never be a real punter because that position, as well as quarterback, was reserved only for Whites.

"Can you punt?" one of them asked.

"I can try," I said.

"You all cannot rush our kicker so you won't hurt him," the White team said. They figured I wouldn't get hurt doing that.

The Black team agreed. They were mostly my relatives and friends anyway, so they had no plans to rough me up.

One of the players on the White team, Chris, said, "Nate, when you hear me yell 'fourth and long,' you come in and kick."

After showing me how to punt, they let me in and I made my best effort, which showed a lot of raw leg power yet needed lots of practice. Each time I heard "fourth and long," I excitingly ran in and gave it my best shot. Fourth and Long became my weekend name, which I came to accept and love. I wanted to get better, so I asked my mother to buy me a football.

That didn't go over too well because my older brother wanted a basketball, but my sisters wanted a tetherball. We got a tetherball ball to share. The problem with that was I couldn't punt the tetherball, which was made of soft rubber, for fear I would burst it.

Determined to practice more, I made a kickable ball out of anything I could get my hands on. Old discarded milk bottles proved to be too hard, and bags filled with dirt made too big a mess that my mother scorned. So occasionally I would sneak and kick the cheap tetherball, and it developed a serious knot for which I was blamed and punished.

I suffered many serious foot injuries because nothing was exempt from my kicking practice, not even no. 303 cans (twelve-ounce cans that fruit and vegetables come in), balloons filled with water, wrapped-up rags (which proved to be the best when taped tightly together), or rubber from inner tubes—I tried anything that could be filled with something.

Upon entering the fifth grade, my parents bought a new home in another community a few miles away. After getting adjusted to the new surroundings, my mother began allowing me and my brothers to go to the park around the corner. Football was the sport of choice for most boys in that neighborhood.

Even as a large strong boy, I was still only a fifth grader and considered to be too young because they were older boys, so I wasn't chosen for teams there either. But that quickly changed one day when the boys were playing another game, with a real football, called put-back. Put-back is where everyone on a team of five or six gets the opportunity to throw the ball at the opposing team, trying to back them into the end zone, which could be any premarked spot behind each team.

The object of the game was to back your opponent into their own end zone before they did it to your team by throwing the football as far as one could, hoping no one on the other team would catch it before it went to their end zone.

I quickly discovered that I couldn't throw the ball as far as most of the boys, who had been playing the game for years, so I asked if I could kick the ball instead. Knowing that kicking was hard to do, they laughed and allowed me to do so, which proved to be their undoing. I routinely was able to punt the ball over their heads, putting them back farther.

After that everyone who had a team would choose me first. My reputation as a punter grew, as did my ability to produce longer and higher kicks. After much begging, I convinced my mom to buy me my very own football, and my world was changed because now I was able to practice, practice, and practice.

For the next three years, my kicks got better as my legs got stronger from practicing and running.

Chapter 2

Learning The Game

In 1963 I started at Booker T. Washington High School as an eighth grader. During play periods and gym classes, I was seldom picked to be on anyone's football team because I just didn't know the rules nor the game. Most of the boys from that very small community, which had only one main street, chose to play one sport or another. I, not being sure of my abilities, chose to be in the high school band and ended up with seventh-period band class on my class schedule.

Catching the Coach's Eyes

About one month after the start of school, some of my friends and I were on the practice football field at the school's back door playing put-back, and there were students watching because it was before first period started. There were also the ever-present eyes of coaches hoping to discover unknown talent, whether throwing or catching a football.

Minutes before it was time to go to class, the ball was thrown to my team and I happened to catch it and quickly return it with a hard high kick, end over end, which sailed into the street behind the practice field about sixty-five yards away. The head football coach, who had started to walk away to go to his first class, heard a thunderous-sounding kick and turned just in time to see the ball sail over the fence and into the street. He turned to the watchful students and other coaches with whom he had been talking and asked in a loud, excited voice, "Who is that fool? Look at the horse thighs on that fool!" All of the boys who were playing in the game had gym class first period, so we were in gym shorts.

"Somebody find out who he is and meet me in the locker room. I don't care who, but somebody!" And he headed that way.

"Who's he talking about?" I asked, even though all the boys were looking at me. Then we all went to gym class.

Afterward I showered and went to my second-period class. About half the class period had passed when two loud-talking men and two students walked into the classroom.

"I need to talk to this fellow," one coach said to the teacher.

"Okay, Coach," she said.

He then walked over to me and asked, "What class do you have during seventh period?"

"I'm in band class then," I said.

"Not anymore. I'll bring your new class schedule to your next period classroom," the coach said.

From Band to Football

I was in third-period class when that same coach, two football trainers, and one counselor walked in, and the counselor presented me with a new class schedule where the seventh-period class was changed from band to athletics.

When I arrived in the locker room at seventh period, I was

greeted by a trainer, a center, and two receivers from the football team, who told me to get dressed in gym clothes and meet them on the field.

When I got there, the center marked off fifteen yards and said, "Let's get with it. We only got one hour before football practice starts."

For the next two and a half weeks, I was instructed to work with the JV center to get ready for their first game. His snaps were lofty, easy to handle, and presented no problems for even someone like me, who had never played in an organized football game before.

On the evening of the first game, as the team warmed up, many were already whispering about this new eighth-grade kicker who could really boom it.

During the first two series of downs, our offensive team moved the ball across the fifty-yard line and scored one touchdown and a field goal. The placekicker was also the JV quarterback, who was very good; he was a boy who lived only about three-quarters of a mile from me, in the same community but a separate division called Hillside Manor.

However, on the next series of downs, we failed to get a first down and I had to punt. It was a disaster. When the center snapped the ball to me, I mishandled the snap because I was not used to being rushed by the opponent. I all but freaked out when I saw all these boys rushing toward me, and I juggled the ball and had to run with it but was tackled behind our line of scrimmage. Lucky for me, we had a great defense that didn't allow the other team to score a touchdown, and they went for a field goal and made it.

The next time we had to punt was late in the third quarter, and while I was back to receive the snap, the ball sailed over my head. I had to scramble to pick it up and began to run with it. I almost picked up the first down, but the ball went over on downs to the other team. As I walked to the sideline, the JV coach grabbed me by my jersey and yelled, "Why didn't you kick the ball, son?"

"It went over my head," I said.

"No one rushed you; they were playing for a return! You need to keep your mind on football, son," he said.

Well, the thing was I didn't have a football mind because nobody ever taught me the game. I literally learned by the seat of my pants. . . though it was more like *on* the seat of my pants. You see, I attempted to punt twice in the fourth quarter, and both were blocked because I was taking far too many steps before kicking the ball and didn't know it until the varsity punter said, "I can't stomach watching you another game!" He then offered to help me.

My Punting Mentor

That following Monday at practice, the head coach came to me and said, "You will work with our varsity punter for a few days until you get some courage and a shorter step routine."

I had watched this guy kick in games, and he was awesome. I once saw him in practice lay a football on the ground at about a thirty-degree angle and kick it into a perfect tight spiral. I tried it for years and never got the tight spiral, though I got off some incredible kicks.

There was a bit of a twist added to my practice routine when the coach sent over a defensive end and a defensive back to rush my kicks to help me improve my steps and timing. They were instructed to lightly push when they reached me, to improve my courage and confidence. I would not be hit hard . . . unless I fumbled or juggled the ball, in which case they were glad to do so. Ray, the varsity punter, drilled me with a one-and-a-half step routine—I had been taking three to four steps or whatever it took to get me into a good enough position to kick the ball. Ray drilled me, like it was a dance step I was trying to learn, until I mastered it. With his coaching, I had to find a way to explode all my power into the kick with fewer steps.

And I did. My newly learned ability to put-back the opposing team with my leg gained me recognition I never knew could be possible for me.

By the time the JV season was winding down, my new friend and kicking coach, Ray, had some legal issues and was unable to stay in school. After watching my development as a punter, the coaching staff had a plan to move me up to varsity. Ray's brother was the varsity placekicker. The school board athletics division bitterly disputed that plan, citing that the insurance liability was too great to have an eighth-grade boy competing against some boys who were almost men.

The great thing for me was that I was allowed to dress for the rest of the varsity's home games but not allowed to travel out of town with them. I was even allowed to warm up before the games but not to play.

Ray's brother assumed his punting duties for the rest of that season.

Chapter 3

Moved To The Varsity Team

The following year, having played offensive and defensive end at 6'1" and 190 lb. as well as kicked for the JV team, I was immediately moved to varsity as starting defensive end, backup defensive back, and backup punter, all as a freshman. Over that prior summer, I practiced everything Ray worked with me on: take one and a half steps, ignore the rushers, and focus on the proper ball drop, both height and position.

Challenges

Being moved up to varsity brought on new challenges and expectations from the coaches and my teammates who were depending on me to get or keep the defensive team out of bad field positions on fourth and long or fourth and short.

Along with this new challenge also came new popularity with benefits. Many girls began to notice me as well; one in particular became my new girlfriend that year. She was not only a senior but also president of the senior class and valedictorian, and she had her own car, a new Barracuda. She learned very quickly that I was not allowed to go riding after 10:00 p.m., which proved to be too much of a strain on the relationship.

But I was up for the challenges and expectations. I had a great instructor in Ray, and I began to master all the different kicks he taught me except one, the tight spiral from the ground.

That summer my greatest challenges came from staying out of trouble and surviving life. You see, I was rapidly becoming a product of my environment. One of my closest friends was my neighbor, who had a brother a few years older than he and I.

Being a high school dropout, he spent a few episodes in juvenile detention. During his time in custody, he learned that he had to defend himself often and became a feared fist fighter. He would tease me, saying I was a cutie and had better learn how to fight. I didn't think that would be necessary and refused, but he would not accept my protests. He would playfully hit me in my chest with his fist as hard as he could, which would bring tears to my eyes. I was only a fifth grader at that time.

He'd tell me that if I cried or showed fear to anyone, I would surely become someone's girlfriend. That changed the way I thought, and I let him teach me how to not just fight but box, and I got very good at it. I started going to the YMCA and trained for Golden Gloves boxing. I was later told by the football coaches that if I didn't change my friends, I would be scratched from the team. I would not discontinue my friendship—heck, he was my best friend's brother. I was kicked off the team, but I became a formidable fighter at a young age. Later that season my friend got in some trouble, went back to juvenile, and I was reinstated on the team.

During that same summer, I was told by my mother that I was too young to go to a party. Determined to go, I went as soon as she left and my father fell asleep. I was stabbed, almost fatally, at that party while protecting my older sister from being beaten by a twenty-two-year-old man when she refused his advances. Then I got a new nickname, the Unkillable, which was far from reality.

Although I lived through it, I quickly realized the thug life was not for me. But I could not escape its constant beckoning—most of my close friends were older than me and were thugs.

Summer and Start of the School Year

Being determined to beat the thug life, I worked all summer at a local grocery store and deli as a stocker, cook, and butcher's helper, but I was always careful to get my kicking in. Before summer break, the varsity coach had given me a new football to practice with.

All summer my practice routine was very high impact. I would kick the ball from a spot and run to see if I could catch it myself because my hang time was great. I would repeat it until my right leg was almost numb, then I would kick with my left leg. I tried some kicks on the run, to the right and to the left. But running to the left and kicking with the right leg proved to be a serious challenge, so when I ran to the left, I would actually kick with my left leg. Never considering that I might have to pull this off in a game situation, I only did it to give my right leg a break. My practice would sometimes go on until dark or until my parents called me in.

One month before summer break was over, our football training camp began. A few times during practices, I ran to my left and kicked the ball with my left leg. Everyone who saw me do it warned me to stop clowning around and stay serious about what I was supposed to be doing. I tried to plead my case, that one day I may have to do it, but that was met with even harsher rebuke. Therefore, I wouldn't work on it until regular practice was over, but even then, I was chastised about it.

During my freshman season, the coaches also tried me in practice and games as a fullback, defensive back, and wide receiver. I showed potential in all positions, being very fast with decent hands as a receiver, but playing defensive end got me my first high school letterman jacket. I had several bad kicks in games because of my inexperience, yet my potential outshined those poor ones because of very high and very long kicks that helped to preserve some games. Receiving my football jacket as a freshman set the stage for me to be a four-year letterman, which was not common except at some very small schools.

We finished up that season with a respectable record of winning more than half our games. The coaching staff was quite disappointed—a state title was possible because of our talent level that year, but we didn't get past district champs.

You see, most of our starters on offense and defense were seniors who'd played together for at least three seasons, and some were decorated players with all-state, all-district, and all-area patches. But the greatest disappointment was that we were losing the foundation of our football team. The following season we had to develop many players who were mostly juniors and sophomores with very few seniors who had less playing experience than the rest of the team.

Our new base of starters were now juniors and sophomores, but we were confident that we could get it done. Though we were district champs the prior season, we felt we could go further this year, but the coaches felt we were still in the building stage.

Chapter 4

All-City And All-Area Team Award

During the next season, I was a sophomore and still starting punter and reserve placekicker but now starting defensive end. The previous starting defensive end had graduated the year prior. I was also a reserve fullback now at about 205 lb.

Our so-so season was chugging along—we were winning some games and losing some but not coming close to where we were the season before.

Having an Impact

And yet I was quickly developing a reputation for having the strongest leg in the entire city and area among all the high school punters of any color. During that season I learned what I had to do to avoid dangerous kick returners, kick against strong winds, and handle teams who had good kick rushers. I was even developing a great football mind, now having the ability to produce when I needed to, working up special kicks with the ball and actually pulling them off.

During that time in football history, the coffin corner was the kick of choice to avoid returns, but it was a high-risk kick. It required a punter to line up behind the center, receive the snap, turn to the left or right, and punt the ball so it would avoid being caught by the returner and instead go out of bounds before crossing the goal line. A lot depended on the snapper getting the ball to the punter quickly and accurately, which was less than a 40 percent proposition because as he snaps the ball, there's a defensive lineman or linebacker over him, trying to knock his teeth out before he completes the snap. This made a lot of young snappers very nervous during the cadence.

During summer sessions before school started in 1965, my sophomore year, the snapper who played B team with me was moved up to varsity and was now a junior. His snaps were as hard as a quarterback's pass, throwing a tight spiral at me from fifteen yards away, which proved to be a great asset to our punting game. As a matter of fact, the first snap I received from him at practice broke through my hands and hit me in the stomach, very hard. That brought out some snickers and concerns, so the coaching staff instructed us to work together for the first half of each practice session.

A Snitch in Our Midst

One day on our way back to the school from the practice field, about a half mile away from the school, someone lit a cigarette and offered puffs to several of us who had been dabbling with smoking cigarettes, pipes, and cigars. But wouldn't you know it, there was a tattletale among us. The next day after practice, the coaches called about five names to step forward and let everyone else go. They told us why we were called out and instructed us, one after the other, to lay on the ground under one goalpost and roll to the other one, 120 yards away and back. Five times we had to do it.

When some began to get sick and throw up, they were sent to the showers, but they took the remainder of us (two of my friends from my community and me) to the gym and left, making us run around and around until they returned. Over an hour and a half later they came back to see us still running and singing, so they sat on the bleachers for about thirty minutes watching us. My friends began to cough and stumble and were sent to the showers, but they kept watching me until one coach looked at his watch and said, "This fool is going to make me miss my dinner."

"Not me!" the head coach said. Then he said to the other coach, "He's running around my gym like a darn deer in the forest and having a good time doing it!"

He came to me and said, "Son! Stop! Go home and never let me ever hear of you smoking again, got it!"

"Yes, sir," I said, proceeding to run home about six miles away. They didn't know that I ran to and from school almost every day because my parents, having three kids in high school and one in junior high (and two were girls), couldn't afford bus cards for all of us, so I opted to run. But I never let them catch me smoking again!

An Unexpected Change

My sophomore year was quite eventful. During a scrimmage at the beginning of the year while playing defensive end, I tackled the starting fullback who everyone knew was undersized for that position but had much heart. The next day we were informed that he suffered a broken ankle. I was summoned from one of my classes and told to come to the locker room, where I was informed of his injury.

The head coach looked at me and said, "We're screwed if you can't learn all these plays by Friday."

You see, I was the backup fullback, but I seldom practiced it because of my other positions. Though it was already Tuesday, I learned all the plays that I didn't already know, being drilled all day, every day at school and practice. Wouldn't you know it, I gained over one hundred yards playing against our district rival, I. M. Terrell of Fort Worth, and began to be the go-to guy for needed yardage. But I never got into the end zone—they would always give the ball to the junior halfback or throw a pass when we got close to the goal line.

My punts for the rest of that season kept getting us out of hole after hole and kept our opponents in terrible field position, helping us reach the district playoffs. We were eliminated by an inner-city rival, Lincoln High School, and their star full-back/halfback, who went on to play in college and eventually for the Dallas Cowboys.

During the course of our game against Lincoln, I had the (not so pleasurable) opportunity to tackle this star running back. The first time we met head-up in the zero hole, and I felt numbness throughout my entire body. Though I had reservations about having to do that, I made the sacrifice again and again, each time regretting it afterward. After hitting him about ten or eleven times, I realized that if I was going to last the whole game, I was going to have to find a less painful way to tackle him.

I began to clothesline him, which made him furious because it was as unpleasant to him as tackling him head-up was to me. At the time I was only about 205 lb. He was 6'2" and about 230 lb.

From that point he looked for me instead of looking for his run pattern, which took him off his game. During that time, clotheslining was legal but not for long afterward. But I lived to fight another day!

The season wasn't a total loss for me because as a sophomore kicker, I was named to the All-City and All-Area Teams as first team punter, something no other Black kicker, not even the great Ray, had accomplished before.

One of our preseason games was against Wichita Falls, whose star running back was one of the state's top three sprinters in the one-hundred-yard dash. Three times I caught him from behind, preventing him from scoring on us. I had no idea that our running back coach at that time, who was also the head track coach, took close notice.

When track season started, I was told to run the two-hundred-yard dash. I was too large to run the one hundred but strong enough for the two hundred, yet track was not in my heart as was football. At practice, I proved that I could run with the best two-hundred-yard runners but on meet days, I could not find the heart for it, which was a strange turn of events. You see, as a child I was a runner, and a fast one. I used to outrun all my peers, even my cousin, who by this time had established himself as the top two-hundred-yard dash man in the state.

During one meet we both ran in different heats and would have met in the semifinals if I had not been eliminated in the first round because I could not feel a purpose for running like that for a ribbon or a medal. Now let me chase someone who was carrying a football—that's purpose! The coaches were disappointed that I didn't like track, but besides, I had to get a job to help my parents take care of us.

Our next football season was expected to be much more rewarding with the development of all our underclassmen starters.

The irony of it was that I was from the smallest area in the district, Arlington Park, with only one main street and one-way entrances on both ends of that street.

Yet half the team's lettermen were from that little community. In fact, the entire starting backfield, all the starting receivers, and both kickers were from Arlington Park. We were riding high in anticipation of the next season.

Chapter 5

It's A Homecoming Bashing

For the last home game of the season, our homecoming game, I was appointed as one of the captains for the coin toss. The team was allowed to go home that day at lunchtime and return in time to dress before the bus left for the stadium. Fate can sometimes be cruel, though. I was riding with my friend, neighbor, and teammate Donnie.

I kept telling him we needed to go—you see, his brother was to drive us back to school and was cutting the time too thin as it was. Halfway to school, we had a flat tire, which made us even later, and by the time we got to the school locker room, the bus was loaded and everyone was waiting on us. Donnie was one of the starting guards, and I was the starting fullback and punter.

He Didn't Believe the Truth

As I walked into the locker room, the head coach and others just stared at me. He asked with a calm voice, "Why are you late, son?"

"Coach, we had a flat tire," I replied.

"Get yourself dressed in a hurry, okay?" he said.

"Yes, sir!" I said. Then I approached the cage to get my stuff as Donnie walked into the locker room. The coach looked furious, with fire in his eyes. We were hosting our district's most dangerous rival, and he was in no mood for nonsense.

"Where have you been, son?" he shouted.

"Coach, we had a flat tire," Donnie said. The coach, weighing about 275 lb., vaulted over a bench, grabbed him, and began to shake him violently and beat him with his hands.

After a short while, he turned Donnie loose and shouted, "Get dressed and get your behind on the bus!"

As I was exiting the cage, he grabbed me, snatched a cleat from someone's hand, and shouted, "You started that dang lie!" He proceeded to beat me across the back and shoulders with it. Our backfield coach grabbed him and said, "We have to leave now." The head coach pushed me away and shouted, "Just one mistake tonight, and I'll finish this after the game."

At one play during the game, I was sent out of the backfield on a pass pattern and wouldn't you just know, my friend, the quarterback, threw the ball way over my head. In an attempt to get to it, I still reached for it knowing it was far too high. When I walked to the sideline, the coach called me over.

"Nate! What the heck was that?" he shouted with a grimace on his face. "You looked like you were waving at buzzards or something. Don't test me, not tonight, you hear me, fool?"

It was close to halftime, and we were up by three points. On the next play we failed to get a first down, so I was told to punt. We were at our twenty-five-yard line, which made me stand at our ten-yard line.

When the ball was snapped, it sailed just over my fingertips as I jumped as high as I could. I could hear the coach and some players cussing at me for not jumping higher. Someone said, "He's gonna give these people a touchdown before halftime."

Doing What I Practice

As I turned to chase after the ball, it took one of those crazy bounces and hit me in the chest, and I couldn't believe my good fortune. I started to run to my right and saw a defensive back and end crossing the line of scrimmage toward me.

I looked left and saw no one there, so I took off running in that direction, but the left-side linebackers chased me as I approached the line of scrimmage. One of the linebackers zeroed in on me, but by that time I noticed my right foot was on the ground so I did something that no one expected (not even me). I pushed the ball into my left hand, tossed it toward my upcoming left foot, and kicked a career-long punt that sailed over all the receivers who had begun to move up toward me. It landed and bounced toward what ended up being a fifty-eight-yard kick.

Our defense was fired up, and I heard someone on the sideline shout, "Did you see that? He kicked that with his left foot!"

I went from bonehead to hero in the blink of an eye—or the swift kick of the left kind!

After the game was over, I had a great punt average for the day at forty-nine yards, two touchdowns from the backfield, and over one hundred yards rushing. While dressing in our school's locker room after showering, I heard my running back coach say to the head coach while looking toward me, "Coach, I think you should kick his butt before every game." They, along with other players, had a great laugh, although I was indifferent about it.

That was a far cry from what I'd heard from him the game before when the center, who was benched afterward, snapped the ball over my head for the third time. The coach said he should have snapped it through the uprights—they might have given us three points. That loose ball I didn't even try to get, and the other team recovered it in the end zone for a touchdown. What a difference one game can make.

After football season was over, we began to practice for basketball, but apparently, I still had football on my mind. I remember during our first game, a teammate passed me the ball and instead of dribbling it, I tucked it and ran toward the basket for a layup. The entire gym erupted in laughter as I heard someone yell, "Touchdown!"

One of my buddies asked me what the heck I was thinking, and someone else said, "It's obvious he thinks this is a football game."

But in a way, it was symbolic. At the end of the season, I realized that basketball was not for me.

We went into baseball training after that, and I was, of course, a pitcher with an 85-mph fastball and as much control as a race car with three wheels. My dad came to our first game, but I didn't play and he never came to another, saying that I must not be any good. My brothers were great baseball and basketball players, and my dad was great at baseball and football. How I wish that my father had understood that while baseball was his destiny, football was mine.

Chapter 6

The Bounty On Me

Our football team had high expectations for the next two years because of the team's talent and grit. Most of us had played together for two or three years already, so we were looking forward to a strong season. But sometimes fate will change everything, as it did with us.

An Unwanted Change

I was now a junior in high school and half the team's starters, on both offense and defense, were from my community. But unexpectedly the district line was changed and redrawn, forcing the students in our community except seniors to be sent to a newly built high school, L. G. Pinkston, about four miles away.

I felt that I had too much to lose, as did the coaches who trained and developed my skills and gifts as a kicker and running back. Realizing what had happened was going to ruin our football team, I, with my parents, set up a meeting with the school board of education. I tried desperately to convince them to allow me to stay at Booker T. Washington but to no avail; they told me the only way it could happen would be to have someone's address in that district as my place of residence, but I had no friends or relatives willing to take that risk.

We tried for weeks to find a way but with no success. So, I did the next best thing—since football training had started, I went to practice with the new team at my new school. When some of my friends and coaches heard of what I'd done, I was labeled a traitor, and a bounty was put out on me—they would do whatever they could to take me out of a game by hurting me.

The coaches, my friends, my neighborhood buddies—they didn't believe I had exhausted all possible measures to stay at Booker T. Washington. The irony of it is that some of the other players who lived in my community found out after school started that Booker T. Washington's coaches were not able to keep them either.

Very early I established that I would be the team's new punter. Though I'd just come off my best year as a fullback, I was not going to take the job from a boy who was a backup the prior season. I was from a rival community and was considered a hoodlum, but so was half their team!

When jerseys were issued, I was asked what number I wanted and I said number 44. Well wouldn't you know it, one of their players from the prior season became irate and began using profanity, saying that was the number he wanted. Being the new kid on the block, I asked for another number, one that I had at Booker T. Washington, and received it.

By then all the other players from my community who were also transferred were practicing, trying to make the team, but I was the only one to win a starting position, though it was as a kicker and punter. The others were constantly threatened and looked to me for help, since I had already earned the reputation as someone not to mess with.

You see, back at Booker T. Washington, I was in the National

Defense Cadets Core (NDCC), a student base for Special Forces training during the Vietnam War. I was on the rifle team and pistol teams, and I participated in the passing review, where top military brass from Washington, DC, representing all branches of services, came to inspect our training. My squad received best drill squad, and I received best drill squad leader and was promoted from buck private all the way to sergeant major. My next promotion took me to major. I was already rumored to be the next cadet commander of the entire battalion before I got to be a senior, when none had received that honor, except one.

So, I had already established myself to be a better shot than anyone on their rifle or pistol team. As a matter of fact, I was better with a pistol than all of their ROTC program rifle shooters. I guess they figured if they messed with me, they could get shot!

On the first day of school, a grand assembly was held to greet all the students from Arlington Park, and we were asked one at a time to stand and make comments. I stood to address the assembly and said with a loud, clear voice, "I don't want to be here. I was happy where I was, I was a new football captain, and I was going to be the new student commander of the Booker T. Washington NDCC program." Then I sat down.

The principal stood up immediately and said, "That's okay, we need a good kicker and more players as well, so you're all welcome here. Let's build a great team and win." Then he left the auditorium.

Facing Bounty

About the third game of the season, we were scheduled to play Booker T. Washington High School, and it was very clear that no matter how I pleaded my case, the bounty contract was on and Booker T. Washington coaches were behind it.

Knowing their offense and defensive setups proved to be

very helpful because it seemed as if I always knew where they were going to run and who they were going to throw the ball to. I had great punts that kept them backed up against their own end zone, and though they were favored to beat us by twenty-four points, the game ended in a tie, 10–10.

There were many attempts to injure me, but with hard, clean hits, and I survived them all. Even the players who transferred with me were astounded that they couldn't take me out, but I had to keep my head on a swivel and not get caught sleeping at any moment.

The taunts were constant. "We're gonna get you, Nate! Before this game is over, we're gonna get you!"

They played as though that was their greatest mission that night, taking me out. That may have aided in their inability to not only beat us by twenty-four points but to beat us at all. I stayed alert and stayed tough, with a couple of unnecessary roughing penalties called on me. I was in game mode but had to be in survival mode as well.

This was an insane situation: my old school wanted me hurt, and my new school didn't care. Maybe I said the wrong thing at the auditorium the first day of school. Even my new teammates seemed to not want to forget my desire to not be there, even though I came in and became part of the team.

Trouble on the Horizon

Within the first six weeks of school, I was sent home five times for fighting, but I never started one fight. It was apparent that because I was the most high-profile boy from my community, I was going to have to prove that I wouldn't be bullied.

Being an ex-military student from my previous school, I was allowed to bring my range pistol and keep it in the school's armory and shoot there, hoping to join their ROTC program at the start of the second semester.

One day I was approached by a group of hoodlum players from the football team along with a couple of their thug friends who told me they wanted to see me after school. One of them had an open switchblade knife and threw it between my feet, sticking it into the ground. Well, I'd been stabbed when I was fourteen by a twenty-two-year-old thug and was not about to allow that to happen to me again.

I went to the armory and lied to the instructor, telling him that I wanted my gun and some ammo to practice over the weekend, and he gave them to me. I didn't have a clue of how much trouble I could get that man into, but I walked the halls looking for these guys. The principal happened to see me with my gun stuck into my belt inside my sweater, ran to his office, and made the announcement. "Teachers! Lock your doors, we have a maniac in the halls!"

I saw the guys who threatened me outside the band room cutting class and called them out, but when they saw my gun, they ran out of school and toward the shopping center. I went to my next class, fearful they would return, and placed my gun's barrel in the ink bottle hole in the desk. My teacher looked at me and asked, "What's wrong with you, boy?" I said "nothing yet" in a way that silenced him, so he and the class just sat staring at me until the police came into the room.

They took me to the office and questioned me as to what made me lose my mind. When I told them what happened, they said these boys have always been bullies, but this episode may have taught them a lesson. The police sergeant asked if they should take me to jail and the coaches said, "No, let us handle him."

"Give me his gun. I want to see if it belongs to the school," the assistant principal said. I never saw my gun again. I couldn't complain because my parents didn't know I, being just a junior at that time, owned it.

Meanwhile, the coaches indeed handled it in their own way. I was sent through the belt line, a team disciplinary procedure where there are two lines of coaches and team captains forming a corridor. I had to walk, not run, through the line; they all had belts and beat me. That football season ended.

The next year, which was my senior year, I told them I was not able to attend summer football training because I had to go to work to help my family out. My dad had left my mom, and there were seven children at home and I needed to help my mother. When school started, I was made to go with junior varsity and scrimmage with them because I didn't attend the summer football training with varsity. They saw very quickly what a big mistake that was—I was too dominant for the JV players—and stopped me from participating in football, at either level, for the rest of that season.

That was the end of my football playing for the rest of high school. Later, the coaches, captains, and friends begged me to rejoin the team, but I told them I had to work after school hours to help my family out.

I found out later that when they handed out letters for the year before, when I played as a junior, I was passed over even though I had earned it. I'd heard that the head coach kept my letterman jacket because we had the same last name. I had one of my best kicking performances in my junior year and thought I should have gotten my letter. All the thugs on the team got theirs! Man, I could not believe what was happening to me *again*. Just because the school district line was redrawn, I did not receive my sophomore letter at Booker T. Washington High School either. This was the second year in a row I was not given an award I had earned.

Chapter 7

Dallas Cowboys Tryout as a Senior in High School

First NFL Tryout

During spring break before my graduation, I'd heard of a kicking tryout being sponsored by the Dallas Cowboys and was asked if I had considered participating. Really, I hadn't, but I was persuaded to try out. So, every day after work, I practiced until the date of the tryouts. Running for hours after vigorous calisthenics, for weeks on end, I worked it.

On the day of the tryouts, we met with team coaches, scouts, and sponsors, and I was given the details of the process. There would be three sessions of five kicks, and the five semifinalists would be picked from about thirty contestants.

The semifinal tryouts were held at a local private high school stadium. The placekickers were up first, but I had applied only to punt, knowing that I was less than 40 percent in made field goals from forty-five yards out and I didn't have a chance at placekicking. One of my former high school teammates from Booker T. Washington, who was a senior when I was a sophomore, was there as a placekicker. At school I thought that he was pretty good, because I seldom saw him miss any kicks, but he didn't make the finals.

As a punter I stunned everyone with my leg strength and made the finals. By the conclusion of the tryouts, I had compiled the best record of all the punters. As a matter of fact, the director of scouting marveled over my leg strength, stating, "Such raw power is rare. It sounded as though you hit the football with a baseball bat."

"How old are you?" he asked.

"I just turned nineteen," I said.

"What are your plans for college?"

"I was considering it, but I don't have the money or the support. I've been talking to a local college."

"We wouldn't think of denying you the opportunity for an education. Come see us when you graduate college," he said as his countenance changed.

The experience of outkicking so many professional prospects gave me the confidence to know that I was good enough to perform at that level right then.

During the offseason, besides running and kicking, I did a lot of swimming as a lifeguard and played a lot of basketball, both on teams and one-on-one, which helped to improve my corner cover skills.

College Tryouts

In 1967, before school let out for summer in my senior year, one of the coaches came to me and said, "Grambling University likes what they heard about you as a kicker and a running back and wants you to come down for a tryout.

One year out of high school was when I decided to pursue

college. Through one of my high school coaches, I decided to go to college football tryouts as a walk-on to obtain a scholarship offer at Grambling University as a punter and fullback weighing 220 lb. When I went for summer camp, I was married and it didn't work out after a few games, so I transferred to a local school, Bishop College.

I was introduced to the school's head coach by someone who I was close to at the time that I'd played in junior high and high school, and who had graduated the year before I did.

While working and going to school, I would wake up at three o'clock in the morning and jog three miles to work, work eight hours, and jog back home. Then I would jog three-quarters of a mile to the bus stop to go to football practice for summer sessions until school started.

During camp, I worked out as a fullback, corner, kicker, and kick returner. By the time of the spring game, I was the starting kicker and kick returner and the backup fullback and corner, all as a freshman. The game was titled the exes classic because the team played against the seniors and graduates from years past, some of whom were ex-professionals. I literally put on a punt clinic, keeping the ball away from former kick return All-Pros and other good returners for the first half of the game.

When the second half started, I was called on to return the second half kickoff, and the ball came straight to me on the one-yard line. I made the first two rushers miss, crossed the fifty-yard line down the right side of the field, and looked back over my left shoulder. As I did, I felt a hard chop to the ball, which was in my right hand, that made me fumble it out of bounds. It was a former defensive back from the Kansas City Chiefs stripping me. He did it to me again late in the third quarter, and I was not sent out again to return any kicks.

After a couple of games, it was apparent that this coach

didn't like L. G. Pinkston boys for the same reason as the Grambling coaches. I had one fight and was thrown off the team but later was asked to return and kick. I refused, then later dropped the whole college idea.

That decision cost me a college education. My first major decision in life was the wrong one.

Chapter 8

Semi-Pro Football Changed My Life

The Idea of Starting a Semi-Pro Football Team

At a club one night, I ran into a former fellow L. G. Pinkston baseball team member, Wayne, who invited me to come and work at his place of employment in the machine shop because in junior high and high school, I took machine shop, metal shop, wood shop, drafting, and electronics. I had told him that I'd recently returned home after dropping out of the college scene and wasn't working at that time.

He told me where he worked as a short-run machinist, reminded me that we were in the machine shop class together, and asked if I'd retained anything I learned. I laughed and said, "If you can remember anything about that class, you know that I was the only student who made all A's in there."

While being shown around the entire facility, I was taken to the plastics injection shop and introduced to the machine operators.

One of the men I met went to the same school as Wayne and

I. He had graduated the year before I was transferred there but looked very familiar. I learned that he was my older brother Daniel's good friend, and my brother often talked about him.

I remembered Daniel mentioning this friend, Joe, and others were planning to start a semi-professional football team on the west side, his community, and joining the United Independent Football League (UIFL). That evening, I talked with Joe about it and during our conversation, I realized that I'd played against him and his friends when I was an eighth grader and was moved up to junior varsity. He talked about how his friends had such a hard time tackling that huge eighth-grade fullback at Booker T. Washington.

He stated that he and some of his friends had been playing sandlot ball and were thinking of forming a team and joining the league. I thought that was a great idea and started playing sandlot with them to prove my toughness. They thought I was too aggressive a hitter to play sandlot. I would tackle someone and knock them into the hedges alongside the field on which we played, so I was made to just watch and play offense.

Forming a United Independent Football League (UIFL) Team

It didn't seem fair to me that they could tackle me, but I couldn't tackle them! But I wanted to see what the UIFL and this team were about, so I attended their meetings and get-togethers / beer parties. At one meeting the motion was put on the floor to choose a team name and mascot. Names were suggested for about thirty minutes, and I threw out the name Bandits. The West Side Bandits! I liked it. We voted on it and it was so, and the mascot we also voted for reflected the team's name to a T—a man's head wearing a cowboy hat and a scarf covering his nose and mouth. The team colors were unanimously voted to be black and gold.

As we talked, I became more and more interested in this startup team. I was invited to the first organization meeting, which turned out to be mostly a self-bragging session, but another meeting was set for the weekend and I attended.

The first order of business was to see how many potential players were interested. About forty-five guys showed up, mostly guys who didn't get college opportunities, who couldn't make the high school team, or who never played organized football before. A list of positions had been prepared and names were solicited for each.

All the positions had several hopefuls columned under them except the kickers, where there were only two names, one being me. As soon as the other guy was told I was the one who tried out for the local pro NFL team, he withdrew his name. There were no names under the placekicker column, so Joe put his name there, having done some placekicking for the school. Being the team's most skilled tailback, he asked for a backup placekicker hopeful so I volunteered my name, and I eventually won both jobs.

Team captains were selected, and I was one of the few who were chosen. Practices were scheduled evenings after work during the week for two months to access talent and see who would win not only starting positions but a spot on the team.

After about seven weeks, it was apparent who was not going to make the team because they couldn't survive the workouts. Being a workout fanatic, I was told to lighten up or be removed as workout captain. I was eventually removed because I considered a hard workout to be seriously important—apparently more than everybody else!

By the way, I got the job as a machinist and enrolled in and attended a machinist school at TI. I chose machine shop as a skill opportunity to fall back on. While working as a short-run machinist part-time at night and attending machinist school five days a week, eight hours a day, I graduated after six months.

Chapter 9

The Making Of The Bandits

The team was fully organized, sanctioned by the UIFL, and put on the league schedule. We met one Friday to issue jersey numbers to the starters, and the others got the leftover numbers. One unlucky wide receiver was issued the number 77, which usually is a tackle's number. I requested the number 00, which was immediately shut down by the other captains who stated that even though they knew I'd earned two spots on the team, 00 was an earned number. You had to prove yourself worthy of that number by being someone who everyone talked about around the league, so 00 remained up for grabs. I chose 25, which was my number my entire school career, from eighth grade through junior year of high school.

First Game

During our very first game, I played as a cornerback and punter, and we played a team from Irving, Texas, which some of our players were familiar with, having played for them. Midway through the second quarter, we found ourselves being taunted by a team that was considered inferior to us, not only because we were down by a score of 10–0, but we were playing in very cheap, faded, discolored uniforms. Someone needed to step up and quiet the hometown taunting.

We had fourth and long on our thirty-five. I was on our twenty-yard line with a strong wind in my face. Their offense had been pushing our defense up and down the field, and we needed a spark before halftime.

As I lined up for the punt, I noticed the right side was open because they were set for the kick return, and I knew there was enough room for me to pick up the first down so I committed to do it. I knew if I called time-out, they would know something was up, so when the ball was snapped, I caught it and made a half step with my left foot and as I took my right foot off the ground, I made a loud thump sound with my mouth and took off running.

I was shocked to see no one seemed to know what I was doing and didn't pursue until I had a first down. By that time our team started downfield blocking and before I knew it, I was in the end zone, sixty-five yards from the scrimmage line. We lined up for the extra point and I didn't know if I could do it, but my snapper encouraged me to give it my best try, and the ball hit the crossbar and popped over.

When I went to the sideline, my coach said, "I think we have another tailback, a two-hundred pounder."

While celebrating, someone shouted, "We can go in at half-time with a tie or the lead if we can hold them."

With only 1:32 left on the clock, they were on our twenty-yard line and their quarterback challenged me at right corner. I heard someone on their offense tell him I was tired, and I was, so he came at me with a ten and out, their bread-and-butter play, and I was ready.

But I set up in a posture to give him the impression I was out of position and when the receiver cut, I was already moving to his spot. The ball was slightly ahead of him, and I was there to take it. I never broke stride as I caught it and outraced everyone to the end zone, my very first pick-six, and we were ahead by three, 13–10.

I asked the coach to send Joe in to kick but the trainers were working on his ankle. I went in but I was so tired, I couldn't feel my legs. When the ball was snapped and the holder set it down, I made my most valiant try . . . and kicked the ground about four inches behind the ball. My foot bounced into the ball, sending it sailing into the center's jewel pouch, and he screamed obscenities at me. It seems everyone else in the stadium got an enjoyable laugh, though he didn't seem to get the humor.

The coach didn't really know how to react. I had just scored a sixty-five-yard TD and then committed the kicker's cardinal sin of missing the ball, but he gave me a pass for the moment. We went on to score twice more in the second half while holding them to just ten points.

The following Monday at practice, the head coach called me over and said, "You'll never get tired on our team again. First of all, you'll run two extra laps before practice and two extra laps after practice."

He called us up after warm-up exercises and made me do my extra two laps, then paired everyone up except me and led us to the street beside our practice field. He pointed at this old tank of an automobile, a 1967 Buick Wildcat, and said, "First pair, step up and push that car to the end of the block and back."

After going through all the pairs, he got to me, and I asked, "Who's my partner?"

"Me. You push, I guide."

"But what tha hell you mean?"

"Not what tha hell I mean but what the hell I meant. Didn't I tell you—you'll never get tired on this team again!" The levies were north and south hills that border the Trinity River about fifty to seventy-five feet high.

"Man, I know damn well we're not going to do this every day."

"By no means—only twice a week. The other three, the team will run plays, and you'll run the levies—five times."

"Don't you mean four? Over and back twice equals four?" I counted and asked.

"No, over and back equals one—five times."

During the first day of that, by the time my count was at three, I was stumbling up and rolling down the hills. But a month of that and I never got tired in a game again that season, and it set the stage for my personal work ethic.

Second Game

During our second game of that season, we played a team who turned out to be our league rivals, the Dallas Panthers, and many of our players knew someone on their team. They had a player who had just returned from an NFL tryout with one of the California teams and was a very good running back, hard to bring down by most players in the UIFL.

On one particular play, they lined up to try a field goal to go ahead of us late in the game. I was set on the outside of their blocking back and when the ball was snapped, I started to rush. Knowing what a good blocker he was, I jumped to hurdle him and he raised up on his block, knocking me off stride and off balance, and I landed very hard on my tailbone, which hurt like you wouldn't believe. It was a very hard block, which I never forgot.

My next agenda was to get stronger. I began to body build for strength and power rather than muscularity, but I learned they were a package deal. During all our pregame warm-ups, I would start by hitting half-motion kicks to three-quarter to full kicks to ensure that my form was intact. Word of my leg strength and kicking skills had passed through the league. Some of the coaches from other teams would try to discourage me from being on such a young team, stating that my talents would go unnoticed.

On the contrary—some people were coming to games just to see me warm up. Many were scouts from other semi-pro leagues.

The Panthers' head coach was relentless at trying to talk me over to his team. Once I warmed up, I was constantly hitting eighty- to eighty-nine-yard punts, with hang times of five and a half seconds and beyond. It was a show within itself.

During a game in Waco, Texas, I averaged over forty-five yards, with my longest punt being ninety-two yards after the bounce. I had a little tailwind, which the kick returner misjudged, allowing the ball to sail over his head.

Our uniforms were white pants dyed black and cheap black jerseys with iron-on numbers. After the third game, the pants were gray from fading and most of our jersey numbers were coming off. At our next team meeting, we began to come up with ideas for how to purchase new uniforms, good ones that wouldn't fade and with numbers that stayed on. We had won our first two games and lost the third.

Chapter 10

Earning My Stripes

Receiving #00

By this time, one of our organizing players had a new job working for a company in the aviation industry. The owner became interested in becoming a partial sponsor of our team and pledged to help with purchasing our new uniforms.

He became a sponsor and was so impressed by the team's efforts that he not only partially paid for the uniforms, but he also bought new helmets and pads. All players were responsible for our own shoes and socks. We spent a couple of days fitting everyone who made the team, about forty-four players, and passed out assigned numbers. By that time, I had established myself as a team leader, starter on offense and defense, kicker and kick returner, well deserving of the title "impact player," and I received the number I desired: 00.

When the time came for our fourth game of the season, we faced a very tough contending team with four well-known players from Dallas, though the team was from Ennis, Texas. It was a hard-fought game and very strategic. Each team always tried to take advantage of certain players not being on the field and others being tired. There were not a lot of punts. Mostly the ball moved up and down the field on both sides. When it was all said and done, I had twenty-two unassisted tackles from the strong safety position and averaged over forty-five yards with four punts.

"Hey, Coach! Do you keep that 00 beast in a cage between games and feed him gunpowder?" the game announcer asked. Now that was a conversation piece for quite some time.

For our fifth game, we faced a team that was known for their passing game and strong-armed quarterback named Jordan. He tested me from the very start, which proved to be a bad decision for his tight end's sake. He was a monster at 6'6", about 240 lb. Jordan sent him down and across the middle ten yards in front of me. With his size and strength, he expected to catch the ball and run me over, but I slammed him in the chest and stomach as he reached up for the ball.

As I looked into his eyes as I got off him, I thought I saw a tear. That didn't matter because when he got up, he mumbled, "Ain't worth all this." He started undressing and by the time he reached the sideline, he'd taken off his jersey and pads and proceeded straight to his car and left the field.

On the second half kick-off, the returner crossed the fifty and then our forty. In an angular pursuit, I had to dive to catch him, then grab the neck of his jersey (which is now illegal to do) and jerk down while bringing up a right forearm and elbow to his jaw. That almost ended the game, you see—he was knocked out for about ten minutes, and fights were breaking out all over the field because of that hit. I said, "It's part of the game, baby! If you can't stand the heat, get the hell out of the kitchen!" Control was finally attained, and the game was finished.

Facing the Dallas Police Academy

Some of these games quickly broke out into violence because most of the teams originated in the rough part of their town or city, but not all. Some were respectful business owners—even the Dallas Police Academy had a team, which brought about some intense moments. When we played them in our sixth game, there were several scuffles that were quickly brought under control considering all the off-duty security at the game.

I had three interceptions, one for a pick-six, plus two field goals and four extra points, and we won the game, something like 34–21. The police there were very friendly to me the whole game. I had several hits on their 235 lb. star running back and their star sergeant quarterback.

On my way home, I know it was purely coincidental that I got two tickets before I was a mile from the playing field. But on another occasion, knowing that quarterback got me out of getting one ticket after I was pulled over for speeding on the freeway and I was just told to take it down a notch and be more careful.

Before I knew it, our season record was a respectful four wins, one loss, and one 6–6 tie, earning us a slot as a serious contender for the title game. Being good at everything I did, I'd earned much respect by many and a bounty on my head by others. Some of the opposing coaches told their players that if they could take me out of the game, they had a much better chance of beating us. Some wanted it done clean; some would take it any way they could get it, even bounty.

I averaged over forty-five yards per kick with double-digit unassisted tackles. Part of the game of football is intimidation, and I tried to make anyone who caught a pass in my zone pay with his body.

Chapter 11

A Playoff Shot

In the seventh game we played a team from Ferris thought to be the No. 2 seed that year and known for their hard-hitting defense and a 245 lb. tailback. He was a well-known player from his junior high school days but was now in his mid-thirties, still running over kids.

When I met him before the game at the fifty-yard line for the coin toss, I realized that he played when my aunt was in high school. He tried to intimidate me by telling me to look for him because he'd be looking for me.

One particular play, they handed him the ball and we met head-on in the zero hole, and it sounded like a truck wreck. I hit him about waist-high with my head, both of us stopped dead in our tracks, and he said, "Nice hit, feller." I tried to look as unscathed as possible, but my neck and shoulder felt as though I'd hit a cement wall.

There were several attempts to block our punts because they had a false scouting report that said I took too many steps before getting off my kicks. They were no more successful at it than anyone else we played. The wind was blowing about fifteen to twenty miles per hour, making kicking into the wind a chore for most, but I handled it quite well. Late into the second quarter, we were backed up deep in our own end of the field, and I was standing on our two-yard line facing a brisk wind.

I noticed that the return men were playing me quite shallow as they lined up on our forty-five-yard line. My mastery of the punt had to be at its best in this situation. So instead of a normal waist-high drop, I released the ball a little lower than knee-high with perfect ball placement on my foot after my usual one and a half steps. They expected the ball to be a high wind-lifted floater, but I drove a tight spiral line drive about fifteen feet high that pierced the wind like an arrow and went zooming over their heads. The ball landed on about the thirty-five-yard line on their end of the field and bounced straight up, landed, and stopped before it was well covered by our special team players.

I had hit the ball on the five-yard line into a twelve to fifteen mile an hour wind with no return. When you tack on another ten yards where the line of scrimmage was, I grossed a fifty yarder off the toe. The entire crowd went nuts because they couldn't believe what they had just witnessed. That night in five punts, I averaged forty-five yards with only one return for fifteen yards.

When the game was over, we'd squeaked out a three-point win. We had a bye the next week, and some of us went to scout our next opponents. Well wouldn't you know, I'd see that tough tailback at that game, and he looked at me with that same grin as he did when he knelt on my chest the week before.

"Nate, I knew you were hurt when I looked deep into your eyes," he said, shaking my hand and grinning.

"Is that so?" I asked. "So why didn't you ask for the ball on the next play?"

"I also know your heart and knew that you would hit me just as hard. I was hurt that play as well but wouldn't admit it at the time. Besides, I've been watching you for some weeks now, and

I knew you would not shy away from the personal sacrifice or challenge." He looked at the guys I was with and said to them, "This is the only person in this league that I fear for his hitting."

Avoiding Dangerous Return Man

In the eighth game as a kicker, I had to face one of the most dangerous return men in the league. The wind was very brisk, but I had to come up with a way to work the ball away from him. Once he lined up on the left side but the wind caught the ball and floated it straight to him, and he scored on us.

My team and coach were pissed at me because that tied the game, but I didn't know how I could have done that, as much as I had practiced my different kicks. I couldn't blame the wind; I just missed my drop area and said it wouldn't happen again.

"If it does, we could lose," Coach said.

There were only three minutes left in the game, we'd moved the ball to their fifteen-yard line, and it was fourth and seven. Our field goal team came on the field, looked at me in the huddle, and said, "This is the game. Make it and we got a shot at the playoffs; miss and we watch the playoffs."

It was a low snap and the holder struggled to set the ball down and all I saw were big white laces, which is something you don't want to see as a kicker. He tried to spin the ball with his set hand still barely in front of the ball about the time I made contact with it. I hit the ball and nicked his hand, causing it to take off lower than usual, and you could see everyone in the stadium holding their breath. An interior lineman jumped and got a finger on the ball and it hit the crossbar, bounced almost straight up, and barely fell over the bar. Our side of the field and stadium went nuts.

As I went to the sideline to get the kick-off tee, no one said a word, not even the coach; they just looked at me in total confidence. Their top kick returner lined up deep in the middle of the field. I knew it didn't matter which side I kicked it to; he was going to get it if it went deep. I couldn't chance it, so I just hopped it over their first line to the left side tight end, saving a runback. They quickly moved the ball across midfield, but we took over on downs. They held us on our end of the field and with the aid of a couple of their time-outs, we had to punt to them.

My Punting Skill at Its Best

I was backed into our end zone with less than a minute to go and needed the kick of the game. Again their returner had a chance for a runback and lined up as though he expected a coffin corner kick. Before the ball was snapped, I saw him move toward the center of the field expecting me to kick it down the middle, which I did except I dropped the nose of the ball on the line of my pinky toe instead of diagonally across my big toe and hit it with a soccer-style sidewinder. The ball started out straight at him and at the last moment made a sharp left fade with the nose straight up.

He tried to recover his position, but the ball was moving left too fast and he misjudged it and fumbled it, and we recovered it and ran out the clock. In the presence of the head coach, our offensive captain running back and quarterback both came to me and said, "You tried to do that! Didn't we tell you not to pull that crap during a game?"

"Hey, it worked, guys!" the coach said. "Hell!" Then he walked away.

I knew then that I was the master of my punts because I spent countless hours practicing different kicks for different occasions. Though I missed on a few attempts to move the ball where I wanted it to go during the next three games, I didn't stop trying to work the ball, and none of my misses cost us.

Well, we made the playoffs by one game that year, and many of us knew where we were as players and knew what we had to do to win the first round, but we lost the game. I received second team as a defensive back and kicker when the all-stars were chosen at the year's awards banquet and was very disappointed because I felt like I was the best.

Chapter 12

Playoff And Women Woes

Falling Short of the Championship Game

In our last regular season game while playing cornerback, I was a tight cover man and got beat for a touchdown for the first time that season. I had the reputation of beating up on receivers, being 6'1" and 200 lb. My number was called by their quarterback and as I came up to hammer the wideout, he slipped my blow and blew past me as I chased him to the end zone. The ball reached him over my outstretched hand as I jumped wide-legged.

At that moment, one of our cameramen snapped the play and posted it on a half life-size scale (thirty-six-inch frame) on his living room wall. We had our meetings all during the offseason at his house. That particular snapshot became my inspiration to never be burned again and for the next three years, I wasn't.

But for the most part, the rest of that season was pointless, as we had discovered that we'd lost our chance at a championship with two ties and one loss.

In one of our ties, we played a team that had at least two

convicted felons who came on the field with weapons, more afraid of the community where our team was based than any particular person. When I heard of it, I put out the statement that if anyone used a weapon of any kind against anyone on my team, that person would be dealt with, and it was a promise that I meant because I came prepared to do just that.

Just before halftime, a serious yet funny thing happened. One of the players had a straight razor in the belt loop of his pants and during the process of making a tackle on our runner, the razor became dislodged and he accidentally cut himself in the side rather deeply and had to receive medical attention.

I don't know if it was the result of that incident or the threatened promise of being dealt with, but I never heard of another episode of weapons being brought onto the playing field again. Everyone knew that I would do it too, if put into that situation.

Having the reputation of starting to drop the hammer at a very young age, I was known as the person you didn't want to piss off. Being a product of my environment, the small town in which I was raised was called the Park or New Jack City. If one jacked with one of us, they had to deal with the whole town. It was a place where drugs and killings were part of life.

I spent all that summer, six days a week every evening, running three miles to a park to practice both placekicking and punting. I punted into the wind with my right leg, jogged to the ball, and kicked it back with my left leg for two and a half hours, then jogged back home. My legs became like steel beams with muscles wrapping across my quad muscles.

A Woman Scorned

By then I was separated from my wife and met a lady from a small East Texas town, a schoolteacher with whom I developed a close relationship. Being separated for a year or so, I was still apprehensive of intimacy, but I was also apprehended by the beauty of her eyes. She was a bit on the skinny side, though, the type of woman I was not attracted to.

By this time, we were very close to the first game of the preseason, and I allowed myself to spend a long intimate evening with her, not considering how important this game was. We prepared for the game all the next day, and that night I unknowingly ignored her, which proved to be a big no-no!

As we entered the stadium for the game, she approached me with the look of a woman scorned. As I asked what the problem was, she slapped me as hard as she could while screaming, "You spend an intimate evening with me and don't speak to me the next day? That is not acceptable!" I tried to explain that my attention was on the game at hand but again, a woman scorned don't hear much of what you say. I was never able to repair the damage done.

As we warmed up before that game, I consciously kicked balls harder than normal, and one of my coaches noticed and told me to settle down and get my head into the moment. "Whatever's wrong, now's not the time to think about it." I had a great kicking game and a respectful game as a corner.

Chapter 13

All-Star Games

Oklahoma All-Star Game

Being selected to the all-star team that year as a starting kicker and reserve corner was a great honor for me. Our bus trip to Oklahoma City was the reward for our long, hard offseason workouts getting ready for a spring game against a farm club for the pros. We sang, joked around, and just got on each other's nerves the whole trip. When we got to Oklahoma City that Saturday evening, our bus was held up by a parade that was a mixed cultural motorcycle gang.

As we watched and waited while the bikers passed, I saw someone who resembled a cousin whom I'd not seen in years. Later, after the game was over, I was met at the end of the field by that guy who turned out to be my cousin.

All the way along the trip, our players boasted about how they were going to play so well against these pro rejects, as they called them. What we all found out was these guys were of pro caliber in every respect—size, speed, and determination—bragging that we shouldn't be on the same field with them.

Though we were made up of the best from UIFL teams, for the most part they were right. After only a few plays, most of our offensive team had all the courage and fight beat out of them. We had a few very good players, but we were mostly weekend ballers with nine-to-five jobs, most of whom were in decent to terrible condition. I was a physical specimen and was bench pressing over four hundred pounds and squatting almost six hundred, with a body fat content of 4 percent. I had the NFL body and skills to match. Some of my teammates could hold their own but had to be reassured.

Our right corner got too scared to play effectively, so I got the call midway through the first quarter. On a lot of plays, I counted at least five blocks thrown at me and yelled that someone had to be open to make some tackles. This made me even more determined, and I made tackles all over the field.

Some of our offensive linemen were beaten up and had no desire to finish, even our two largest, weighing over 300 lb. each. Our defense was holding the scoring down as we went into the fourth quarter down by only six points. On one sweep play, I was trailing the runner across the field from my corner position and as I reached him, I cut back behind the line of scrimmage and darted toward the outside.

About the time the runner cut, a pulling lineman threw a low blindside block, which turned me onto my head. I was then hit by another blocker, probably the fullback. I somehow landed on my feet running and like a blur, I caught the runner from behind on their sideline and took him and a lead blocker out of bounds. Their coach was furious as I heard him screaming and cussing at some of their blockers. "Damn it! I told y'all to lay on him after you block him or just hold him until the play is over."

I limped back to the defensive huddle and said, "Man, it's like trying to cross I-35 during rush hour out there on that field."

I had seventeen solo tackles and seven assists, two interceptions with one a pick-six, and three field goals. My punt stats were great as well with five punts averaging fifty-one yards. I was informed afterward by an Oklahoma fan that I was an object of bounty, hard but clean. A dollar amount was placed on my head, and that was not the first nor the last time I was the target of a bounty.

A young lady came to our dressing room and asked for me by my 00 number, and she invited me to an after-game party. I declined the invite, stating that I had to catch the bus home that night. But she was not to be denied and offered to drive me home the next day. I simply stated, "That would be more dangerous than the game I just finished." I politely brushed her off with a thanks, but no thanks.

While preparing for our next season, we had several meetings / beer drinking sessions trying to figure out what we needed to improve in order to get back into the playoffs. Many of us knew the talent we had and felt that some games were taken from us by a lot of bad calls because we were the newest kid on the block.

A Not So Sobering Moment

In the midst of one of those sessions, a fellow whom I'd never met was introduced to me as a new team member, a wide receiver, where we'd been hurting.

As we sat talking, he pulled out what looked to be a bag of weed, and he and the guys who introduced him to me began to roll and light up joints. I heard them tell one of my teammates, "This is a live wire." They offered me a hit and I declined. They didn't stop offering, claiming that I was too square. I heard one say, "Man, I thought you said this crap was live. Here, Nate, hit this. It's no stronger than a regular smoke." So, I did.

A few moments later, the host wanted us to go outside

because the room was too smoky, so out we went. We sat on cement walls and his brick porch wearing practice shorts and tank tops with flip flops, some in their bare feet. I was asked, "Do you feel anything?"

"Nope, how about you, Bud?"

"Nope."

Everyone who was asked that question said, "Nope, this stuff's bunk."

A wild laughter broke out. The irony was that no one felt anything even though it was drizzling and freezing, about seventeen degrees. So, it was apparent that crap was quite live.

Chapter 14

Bad Karma

A Chilly Day

The next day was a Saturday, the last game of the season. We won the coin toss, and I was the deep return man. It was still drizzling and seventeen degrees. No one wanted to touch the kick because the natural grass field had several half-frozen mud / water puddles. Some were as large as a dining table.

As fate would have it, the kick came straight to me and the only thing I could think of was to get as much yardage as I could and get the heck out of bounds. But when I crossed the fifty-yard line, one of my blockers slipped and fell in front of me and the defensive man hit me from behind, knocking me face down into a large puddle of frozen, wet mud. About four more people just laid on me as I yelled, "Get your butts off me!" I think they just were slow getting up on purpose.

It turned out to be the worst thing I felt all day because my whole body became numb, and I felt nothing else the rest of the game. After I took a hot shower and thawed out, everything was hurting. Both my knees were aching, both ankles were sore, my elbows burned, and my face just throbbed with pain.

It wasn't much longer that I had an acquaintance come to town, and I told him of the team and of that crazy moment before the game, and he just smiled. He said, "I didn't know you did pot."

"That was my first and last time ever," I told him.

During the next few months, I'd moved to the projects and met a guy who told me he'd been to our games and watched the kicking show that I put on week to week, and after a few weeks he and I were friends.

After telling some of my teammates about him, they became concerned for me, saying they wanted me to know that my new friend was a hardcore gangster who'd killed people. As a matter of fact, he'd just gotten out of prison for murder. Little did they know, I'd lived that same lifestyle from the time I was in junior high school and had been shot and stabbed before I was fifteen years old, so I was not scared or intimidated.

I was surprised to see him arrive at our practice field a short time later and drive his car right onto the field. He got out and walked over to me and said, "Man, I'm sorry to disturb y'all's practice, but I need to take care of some business!"

I was shocked to see what he did next. Walking over to our offensive huddle, he grabbed a player, pulled him out of the huddle, and began to beat the crap out of him. I was shocked because this player was one of the community's most feared bullies.

Half of our team were thugs, degenerates, and ex-cons, but no one said a word or did anything. After the beating was done, he walked over to me and said in a loud, tired voice, "If anyone gives you trouble, let me know," and he left.

About a week later, as me and my oldest daughter, who was about six or seven years old at the time, sat on the porch and talked, we saw a man with a shotgun on his shoulder, holding it by the barrel, walk past our unit to the one behind us. When he disappeared from sight, we heard three loud booms and immediately saw the man running through the units. The next day, I moved my family out.

It was about time for our season to start. We played our second preseason game on a Saturday morning and won it 24–0. Some of my close associates wanted to celebrate by finding some women of the night in North Dallas. I said, "I'm afraid that I'm not for that. Let's go to Pappy Dad's instead and get some of those great hot links."

One of the guys scorned the one who had the idea of finding the women, saying, "I don't care what they look like, that's not safe!"

So, we all agreed to go get some links and a case of beer and get back to the west side, which was dry. About a block after we left Pappy Dad's, someone saw the most beautiful woman, standing about 5'10", with long dyed blond hair and gorgeous legs. Surprisingly the fellow who scorned the other guy about finding women of the night screamed, "Please, please stop this car! Can someone please loan me twenty bucks?"

Apparently, he was either a hypocrite or maybe her looks changed his outlook. We had a big laugh on that one, and I said, "Man, get a hold of yourself! That's a lot to pay for an STD!"

Position Change

In our ninth game of the season, we faced the team from Ferris again, with their star safety along with their tough tailback. On our opening drive after receiving the opening kickoff, the ball was constantly fed to the tailback and me, the fullback. Before I realized it, we were on the fifteen-yard line, and I got the call three straight plays and took us to third and goal at the five.

The ball was handed off to me and as I broke through the line of scrimmage, I saw their star safety standing on the one and had it in my mind to go in untouched. When I reached the two-yard line, I faked to go left to get a commitment from him and he did, but when I made a hard cut back to the right, my plant foot slipped and I lost my footing.

By the time I recovered, he had already planted his helmet into my midsection, taking me down short of the goal line. I was asked by an irate offensive captain, "What the heck was that? You could have easily run him over. Why didn't you?"

"I lost my footing." I simply said.

"Well, you now have him and everyone in the stadium thinking that you're afraid of him."

Even though I'd already had over forty yards rushing during the first drive, I didn't get any more touches that game and was reduced to backup fullback. The reason given was that the team couldn't risk losing me as a kicker. I was leading our team in interceptions and batted down passes all over the field yet was not allowed to play cornerback the rest of that season. What the heck—in that game I had punts of sixty-eight, fifty-five, sixty-seven, fifty-nine, and fifty-eight yards for an average of sixty-one point four yards, as well as three extra points and three field goals of less than forty-five yards, and we won the game by six, 30–24.

During the last game of the season against a team from Garland, Texas, I decided to showcase my kicking skills and end the season with a bang. I tied my last game's punting average of sixty-one point four yards in six punts. Along with the other game's stats, it was enough to get me the kicking title and All-Pro honors for that year.

During the offseason I ran like a madman and incorporated some leg weight routines. By the time the next season rolled around, I was in the best shape of my life and stronger than I'd ever been in my legs and upper body but now with flexibility, having done much stretching before and after every workout, five days a week, without fail.

It was the start of our fourth and my most memorable season. At our first meeting of the season, announcements were made for personnel changes. We added new members, including some from other teams who wanted to be part of our growing promise as an elite contender for the league title and others just wanting to be part of something good that came out of our neighborhood. A few more assistant coaches for specialty positions were brought aboard, and we had a new head coach and assistant coach.

Then they got into the position changes. Our starting strong safety was moved to free safety because he was a range player who was not a sure tackler and who shied away from one-on-one contact with strong runners.

I was removed from corner in favor of a newly acquired corner from another team who had made first team All-Pro team the prior season. I played on the same high school team with this guy, and he couldn't make varsity back then, whereas I did as a freshman (and he was a sophomore at the time). I knew this guy was also all cover, no tackling, and I did them both quite well. But politics have a long arm, reaching even into sports. I was concerned and inquired about my position on the team and was told that I would be the starting kicker and punter and would have to earn anything else.

Determined to do just that, I knew there was no one on that team faster or stronger than me. At that time, I had quads and calves that most professional bodybuilders would covet. But even the Bible tells us that jealousy is crueler than the grave. The team's coaches and captains were convinced that I feared a certain player and didn't want to play him anywhere.

Well, wouldn't you know it, our next game was with that

guy's team. Apparently, he had an altercation off the field with one of our players, Goose, over a woman and pulled an ice pick on him and threatened him before the game. The problem boiled over into the game, and many of the thugs on his team got involved. No one on our team spoke up for Goose.

At the opening kick-off, their guy received my kick and Goose tackled him for no return. When he saw who it was, he grabbed Goose's face mask and began kicking and cussing him, and everyone just stood around begging him to leave Goose alone. It was apparent that no one on our team wanted to intervene, so I walked over and said, "Turn him loose, trick!" He looked into my eyes and just stared while letting go of Goose.

During that game I had about five punts, which was typical, averaging a little under fifty yards because the wind was quite brisk when I had to kick into it two times. One kick was less than forty-five yards, but the kicks with the wind helped my average. I was able to keep the ball away from their best return man, who was an All-Pro at that position, because I had hang time that killed runbacks.

During one of their runbacks, I was able to zero in on this guy and nailed him head-on, dropping him where I caught him. Late in the fourth quarter, we trailed them by six, our starting fullback was having leg cramps, and I was sent in for a couple of plays. On the second play the quarterback called my number, and I broke through the line for fifteen yards, moving the ball to the six-yard line.

"Give it to him again," the coach said and called time-out, summoning me and the quarterback to the sideline.

"Are you sure?" the quarterback asked.

"Do you think I'm afraid?" I asked.

"No!" he said. "You might slip again."

"Give me the ball like Coach said, man."

The ball was snapped and handed to me and I saw a safety

blitz coming, and guess who it was? I faked like I was going to cut outside and made a straight move toward him and as he went down after my legs, I half squatted and drove my right thigh into the top of his helmet, and he bowed backward and fell on his back. I made one more step and stumbled into the end zone. He got up and wobbled to our huddle as we lined up for the extra point; his eyes were glazed and he seemed confused. I told the ref that he just might be hurt, and the ref called a time-out and told his coach to come and have someone check him out.

I don't know how bad he was hurt but I did know that my thigh was numb. I was still able to get the ball over the uprights and we held on to win the game. The referee told me that I may have just made some vote points. On our last possession they became frustrated and started a fight with one of our small offensive guards, who at 5'9" weighed only about 210 lb.

Fighting to Stop the Fight

Their biggest defensive lineman, who looked like Magilla Gorilla at 6'7" and about 350 lb., had him on the ground, beating him like he'd stolen something from him. I didn't say a word; I jumped in front of him and threw a right-hand haymaker uppercut, catching him directly on the chin and lifting and knocking him backward. Heck, after that, the fight ended because he was holding everyone else back as if to say, *Y'all don't want none of that!*

After that night I nursed my thigh for the next three days, practicing only my punts. It was a tough way to start the season. Before that game, our starting strong side safety got into some legal problems and was lost for good, and we had no one else who could play it. The coaches decided that they had to recruit from another team, but I threw my hat into the ring. At first, they were not sure, but later they decided to give me a shot with the condition that if I so much as limped, it would be over. I finished that game with four punts averaging over fifty-five yards and twenty-one unassisted tackles. I had more tackles behind the line of scrimmage than the defensive line. After only one game, a buzz within other teams about me being named All-Pro first team kicker and safety began.

Chapter 15

The Art Of Punting

During the pregame I was on the field warming up. I'd hit only two punts that flew in perfect spirals about seventy yards each over the field lights. We were in Waco, Texas, and a local came up to me and said that he was a basketball fan, not football. But he'd heard of this punter coming to Waco tonight who was as good as, if not better than, the great punter who signed with the Oakland Raiders in 1973, who was about a year and a half younger than I was. He said, "Man, I came to this game just to see you kick, and judging by what I just saw, I'm made to almost believe what I heard about you, so do your thing," and then he walked away.

I had only five punts that night. The first was a kick directed toward a return man who had a reputation for dropping very high punts. So I dropped the ball a little above waist-high and gave it a solid kick. It sailed over the lights and he fumbled but recovered it himself on their ten-yard line. He told one of his teammates that he wanted to let it go into the end zone, but it had a side wobble that might cause it to bounce sideways and go out of bounds close to the end zone.

77

The second punt was late in the first quarter with the wind at my back. The return men were playing for a long high-floater so I hit a coffin corner kick to their right, which landed about ten yards in front of them and bounced out of bounds, netting only forty-eight yards, which was at least on my average so far.

For my third punt just before halftime, I noticed their super-fast wideout was back for the return. This concerned me because I was kicking from deep in our own end zone with the wind in my face, though it was only a light breeze. I noticed he was playing me quite shallow, standing on the fifty-yard line, and they were playing for the return, rushing only three. I dropped the ball slightly lower than knee-high and hit a wobbly spiral only about twenty feet high that hit the ground about ten yards in front of him and bounced hard to his left. Being concerned about our coverage team, he tried to catch the ball while looking to get hit, and he did, dropping the ball. When the dust settled and the refs unpiled everyone, we had the ball.

I'd only tried to prevent a runback, but we got a favorable bounce and the ball back. I tried to admit that it was luck, but some of my teammates weren't buying it, so it was what it was.

I only had two more punts that game because we dominated time possession in the second half but finished with a respectful forty-two-yard average, and we were well on our way to the playoffs, which we won to become league champs.

League Banquet

Now we did it—the newest kid on the block was in fact the baddest! Much of our success was attributed to my phenomenal kicking and punting, but equally responsible was my defensive play, leading the league in interceptions, tackles, and scoring. Some of my teammates and I were invited to the league banquet. Rumors were flying around about something that had occurred during the season that had never been done in the history of the UIFL. We couldn't wait to see what it was and which team or which person did it.

Dining was coming to an end and awardees were being called out, but they were almost done and I hadn't heard my name. I knew that I had to make it, heck, at least second team at something. And it happened—the league commissioner, who was a lieutenant with the Dallas Police Department, called out for silence in the room. Everyone settled down in their seats to hear him.

He started out by giving stats for a kicker, then for a punter, and everyone was whispering, "Well, we know who that is."

Then he mentioned the combined scoring with defensive stats. He said, "The league is very proud to have this caliber of player in our midst in scoring and kicking, along with superb defensive skills."

Then he asked my coach to stand and said, "We're proud to present the titles of league's best kicker—first team, and best safety strong side—first team. Mr. Nathan Scott!"

The room erupted with claps, whistles, and yells. You see, I'd already made All-Pro safety second team two years prior and All-Pro kicker first team three years prior, but nothing could have prepared me for that moment.

But it wasn't all celebration. I mean, you could have heard a pin hit the floor at my team's table, then came the cussing and murmuring. No one from my team so much as made a move to congratulate me, not even my coaches. I had just been recognized for doing something that had rarely been done, if ever, in sports history, and all I got from my teammates was resentment. No one even so much as looked in my direction. Some didn't finish their dinner; they just left because no one else from my team got any award that night.

New Team Bus

By this time in our team history, we'd been in the league for five years and decided it was time to purchase a team bus. We found a great deal on an old high school bus through one of our assistant coaches who was a janitor at L. G. Pinkston and a mechanic.

"It's a great deal but needs some repairs," he said.

"Aren't those conflicting statements coming in the same breath?" I asked.

"We can make it work," he replied.

The team spent more to fix that bus than what we paid for it. It still smoked like a steam engine train.

During the offseason our team got an invite to travel to San Antonio, Texas, to play a game that was just a warm-up for the host team, who played in a league that was a step above our league but still below the NFL, but they got regular salaries.

My teammates didn't want to tell me about the game, but they knew they didn't have a prayer without me, so they called. Against my better judgment, I went. The team decided to take the new bus, knowing there could be problems. Well, that proved to be an adventure none of us would forget. It turned out to be a curse and a blessing at the same time.

The game was set for Saturday night at 8:00 p.m., so we left Dallas at daybreak to give us plenty of time to rest, right? Not!

Well, we were about three miles from the stadium when the bus started making this awful noise underneath and stopped. Our coach, after about two hours of trying to get it going, said, "There's a station about three-quarters of a mile away." Meanwhile someone called the host coach and left him a message about our problem. We didn't hear from anyone so we started pushing, uphill and downhill, for almost half a mile.

Broken up into three groups, we pushed. My legs were dead, half from the pushing, the other half from the long ride.

Finally, a wrecker showed up and towed our loaded bus; our coaches had a small bus sent for them. We arrived at the stadium at 7:15 p.m.—the game was scheduled to start at 8:00, and it started on time. We had no time to warm up and I heard players from the host team say, "Man, this is going to be a cakewalk for the first half. These people are going to be stiff for a while!" Little did he know, we had more than enough warm-up exercise.

Game Time

The captains were at midfield for the coin toss and after we had won the toss, our coaches elected to defer. A giant of a fellow walked over to me and asked, "What position do you play, little guy?" while patting me on top of my helmet.

From that point I knew what I had to do. I knocked his hand away from me and said, "Strong safety, trick!"

"Oh yeah! We're going to see a lot of each other tonight. I'm your job; I'm the tight end."

"I promise you will want to change your position before tonight is over."

He caught a pass in front of me on third and long, and I caught him in the chest with my shoulder pads and helmet, and he dropped the ball and had the wind knocked out of him for about a minute. The next time they had the ball, he ran a ten-yard post and the ball was slightly behind him, and I had a sixty-yard pick-six and made the point after touchdown (PAT).

Just before halftime their quarterback called his number again on a fifteen-yard flag to my side toward their sideline. As the ball hit his hand, I grabbed at it, batting it into the air, and began to chase it while bobbling it. I thought I had it secured and hit another gear, but the ball got away from me as I stumbled out of bounds. A young woman standing by the running track threw a large-size cup of soft drink at me. After it hit me in the face mask, she shouted that I didn't need it anyway while using some shockingly obscene language.

I finished that game with one TD, two field goals, a PAT, thirteen unassisted tackles, and ten assists. I had seven punts averaging just under fifty yards. In a game where they were a twenty-one-point favorite, we beat them 20–17, and everyone now knew that we were the real deal.

Chapter 16

More NFL Tryouts

During our summer workouts, we played four scrimmages against other teams in our league. There was a man who visited most of our practices as well as the scrimmages we hosted on our practice field. During one such game, I toyed with some of the receivers because I knew they couldn't beat me while intercepting three passes, returning one for a pick-six.

This man approached me after the game and introduced himself as the owner of a fast-food restaurant across the street from our practice field. He went on to tell me he was an All-Pro NFL tight end and former Dallas Cowboy.

"Of course, I know who you are," I said. "I'm always in your restaurant."

"Have you ever thought about playing in the NFL?" he asked.

"Of course," I replied. "That's every player's dream."

"Then why don't you try out? I think you have everything it takes."

"Wow! Do you think so, really?"

"Yes, you've got speed, cover skills, and definitely the NFL body. How much do you weigh and what do you lift?"

"Well, I weigh two twenty at six one and I bench press around four hundred and squat a little over five sixty."

"I can see you're very fast. What's your forty?"

"Frankly, I don't know right now."

Then he dropped the bomb. "I'd like to be your agent, that is, if you're interested."

"Sounds good, but I can't afford an agent. Besides, my dream is to be an NFL punter," I said, hardly keeping my cool.

"I think you're more than capable of being successful," he said. "Let me put it this way: If you make a team, we'll discuss my fee. If not, you owe me nothing. So let me send you to a couple of tryouts. Dallas has one starting in two weeks, then there's Houston. But you have to cut this league loose; you've got too much to lose."

"Do you really think that Dallas will give me a punting tryout?"

"I'll take care of that. You just get ready for it."

Second Dallas Cowboys Tryout: 1974

The tryout was at Texas Stadium set from prelims to finals. There were about thirty kickers and at least twenty were punters. We were each given five punts with a snapper from the forty-yard line across the fifty. After the first round about fifteen punters were eliminated, but I made the semifinal. Then we were given about six balls and asked to bang it as far as we could. I survived that because three of my balls hit the bottom of the wall behind the end zone.

I made the final two. We were given six balls and given the same instructions. All but one of my balls slammed the wall about ten feet from the ground. My final ball, with about four point eight seconds hang time, dropped about five yards into the end zone.

We were told to hang loose for about an hour. During that time, the other finalist came to me and said that he'd just left the Washington (now Commanders) team tryouts and was warned of a monumental task by one of my homeboys, who told him you have to beat only one punter whose name was Nate.

"You're Nate, I presume?"

"I'm Nate Scott."

"Well, I know none of us beat you. We never came close! Congrats."

People were coming to the field asking for my autograph before a decision was even given. Two of those people were good friends who came out to support me, one a professional golfer and the other a tight end prospect for the Washington team.

Finally, a scout came to me and said, "We decided we'd like to meet with you at the Cowboys office building on Highway 75." He gave me a time and date.

When the day came, I showed up a little early and was greeted by a young woman who said, "Good morning, Rob."

But when I turned to see who it was, she said, "Oh! I'm sorry. I thought you were our wideout."

When I met with the director of scouting, he said, "Nate, I don't think we want to hire you as our punter, but I understand from talking to your agent that you have real serious defensive back skills with speed. Do you have films? We'd like to see some."

I was disappointed and let him know. "My desire is to be an NFL punter. Thanks, but no thanks."

Later when I discussed the issue with my agent, he said, "I really think you still have a chance as a punter. Just get your foot in the door."

"Let's look at another punting opportunity," I said.

By the way, the Cowboys went to the Super Bowl that year and lost. My brothers still scorn me today. I know that I didn't make the best decision for myself, the second time.

Houston Oilers Tryout: 1974

My agent sent me to the Houston Oilers tryout camp the following week. When I got there, I was told to dress for tryouts. I was given five balls to kick while some early-show veterans looked on. All my kicks were at least seventy yards off toe and over the top of the practice field lights. I saw veteran players high-five each other while hearing some say, "I think we have the fourth down weapon we've been needing."

After about the second day, the head coach walked up to me and said, "Shower and meet me in the office."

I showered and waited for over two hours. Finally, I was asked, "Who you waiting for?"

"The head coach. I'm Nate Scott."

"Oh! You're the one an agent was talking about. Give me a few minutes."

Well, after another hour I was told that he'd left camp, and it wasn't known when or if he might return.

Now the actions with the Oilers were very different than the Cowboys but the results felt the same. Rejection, not for who I was but who and what I represented: a Black NFL punter!

When I first returned from the Houston Oilers tryout, I visited my high school alma mater, L. G. Pinkston, when the football team was practicing. My old kicking coach there asked if I would come and coach their punters, but the head coach, knowing only that I did not graduate college and did not get an NFL contract, rejected the idea.

I later saw someone I played against who saw me kick and

punt for years. He asked if I would come to their practices, which was at Franklin D. Roosevelt High School, to help with their kickers, and I went. The varsity kicking coach said, "We don't need help. Let him help the JV kickers," and I did for the remainder of their preseason workouts. Before the first half of the season was over, the JV kicker had won the varsity kicking position.

Now where that JV to varsity kicker went after high school, I don't know, but I do know that he had the leg and the skills to at least make it to the NFL tryouts.

I was later asked to be an alternate speaker at their high school's athletic banquet, but the primary speaker showed up. Had I spoken at the banquet, my closing statement would have been to the kickers in particular: "Never stop dreaming, never stop kicking, because someone is going to see you and notice your skills."

Chapter 17

Bad Decisions

After the Houston Oilers experience, I discussed the matter with my agent and he said, "I really thought the league was changing in all of those related matters. Sad to see some teams not willing to make the changes. Nate, there'll be other opportunities, so give me a chance to work on some other teams. It's too late for this season, so hang loose but stay away from minor league ball. Just don't take those chances."

Personally, I thought I needed to be better and stronger in my legs, so I decided to give it one more season. But once again my team didn't much care for me as a player—they decided to change my position from strong safety to middle linebacker or noseguard. *What!* I thought. *Are you kidding me? After the best season this league had ever known!*

Starting with a New Team–the Panthers

I decided that the only way I could showcase my talents and get better was to go to a team that had always wanted me, so I called the Panthers' head coach. He said, "Nate, we all know how good you are, but you'll have to come over and earn any spot you want."

So I did, becoming their starting strong safety and starting punter. I didn't pursue the PAT nor field goal kicker spot. But the coach warned that it wasn't going to be easy.

"Nate," he said, 'I'm tickled pink to have you finally, but you know it's not going to sit well with your old team."

"Let me worry about them," I replied. "So here I am a Panther now, right?"

Once our first game was set, revenge and resentment filled the air. There we were standing on the fifty-yard line for the coin toss, me and the captains from both teams and refs who'd be calling the game, all with an unusually thick atmosphere of hate and disrespect for each other.

You see, last season I played for that other team. The coin-tossing ref greeted all the captains individually. One of the other team's captains looked me in the eye and asked, "Nate, you sure you want to go through with this?"

"It is what it is, Black!" I replied.

Then the ref came over to me and asked, "How do you feel, 00?"

"Ref," I said, "as much crap as they've been talking, I don't even want to get along with you tonight!"

The coin was tossed and they won, so I had to kick off.

I heard D. R., one of my alleged close buddies who was also ticked off at me for changing teams, say, "Kick it to me, trick, so I can run it down your throat."

"You touch that ball," I replied, "and your butt is mine, and you know it!"

When I lined up to kick off, I looked for that short piece of crap, but he wasn't on the field—a newcomer to their team was instead. I knew him to be one who couldn't run to his left, so before I kicked, I shouted to my teammates, "Shut off his right and force him to go to his left." I kicked the ball straight to him, and he ran to his left but cut up the middle and broke through our wedge, and I had to catch him as he made it across the fifty to our forty-five-yard line.

I had heard that they had acquired a league All-Pro tight end who moved to Dallas from Oklahoma, and I knew they were going to try me a lot because I played strong side safety, and my job was to cover the tight end. He was huge, about 6'4" and 260 lb., strong as a bear, and could catch. Their first play was an eight-yard down-and-out flag to him, and I hit him as he caught the ball and both of us were stopped in our tracks. I had to wrestle him out of bounds. On second and two, they handed the ball to D. R. and I stopped him at the line of scrimmage. That ticked him off and he yelled, "I'm gonna keep coming at you, traitor!"

I just laughed in his face. "I want you to, chump."

For the first half I single-handedly stopped all their attempts, forcing three and outs. Our offense was having a little better of it, making about five first downs, and I kicked two field goals and we led the first half 6–0.

Coming off the field, there was a lot of name-calling, profanity, and just total disrespect from each team. We were hoping for a playoff spot later and tensions were already high. The fact that I had left that team because of jealousy was gasoline on an open fire.

As we lined up for the start of the second half, it was our ball and I was back to receive and heard someone from their sideline shout loudly, "Kick it to the traitor and we'll take care of him." I knew that would be their plan, so I called a receiver pitch back.

I received the kick and everyone on their team, because of their desire to get me, left the zones they were to cover and made a straight line to me. I ran left and handed the ball to a very fast wideout coming in behind me going the opposite direction, and he ran it to their twenty before being caught.

I walked by their sideline and laughed, saying, "I knew how dumb y'all would be." I was called all kinds of names. They held us to another field goal. At this point I'd all but single-handedly shut down their high-scoring offensive machine, and they grew desperate for change and began to talk about taking me out.

"We're gonna get you the next time you touch that skin, chump."

"Good luck, trick," I shouted. "Because I will be touching it a lot more."

I heard one of my old friends, who actually birthed the idea of the team years ago, shout, "Whatever it takes, you won't walk away from this game!"

"Let's keep it clean, guys," the ref intervened.

"Yeah! It'll be clean all right," D. R. said.

It was eleven minutes into the third quarter, and we had fourth and long from our thirteen-yard line. In the huddle I said, "They're too strong on offense, we can't give them a short field, we got a nine-point lead, so let me run it."

My teammates agreed and as the ball came to me as I was back to punt, they'd expected me to kick it deep, as I'd done for three quarters, but I didn't. I took one step, made a thump sound with my mouth, and ran left. I crossed the fifty, then the forty down to their thirty-five, and was forced out on their sideline.

As I taunted and laughed, pointing at the spot where I went out of bounds, I said, "That's a first down."

Immediately someone hit and grabbed me around my waist. It was my buddy Beetle, and someone coming behind the play said, "Hold that fool up!" while diving into my knee. Someone else did the same from the side, and I saw D. R. and Big Dell get up off me, laughing.

"I told y'all to keep it clean!" the ref shouted, throwing his flag.

I jumped to my feet, took two steps, and my right knee failed and I fell forward onto my chest. Rolling over I felt an enormous pain in that knee and heard cheering from their sideline. My bench emptied to their bench and the refs had to break up the melee.

I couldn't stand on the leg because the knee felt displaced. A friend who'd played at Booker T. Washington with me as a senior when I was a freshman varsity end came over and checked my knee.

"Damn, Nate, you knew this might happen. They said they were out to get you, man. Why the heck did you play anyway?"

"It's just football," I said.

"Hell no, man, it was bounty! They had bounty on you, and you knew it. Me and Shala are going to take you to the hospital. Baby, go get my car."

On the way there, he hit a bump. My knee shifted as I lay in his back seat, and I about crapped my pants. All I could say was, "Where's my Corvette, man?"

"Your buddy Harold said he'll keep it for you."

"Noooo! Not that fool, man!"

Arriving at the hospital, I was seeing images of crabs in a bucket, pulling those trying to escape back into the bottom.

At Dream's End

Hours later I was assigned to a private room and spent more hours waiting to be seen by a doctor or nurse or someone. A nurse finally showed up and asked me questions about what happened and let me know I would be scheduled for X-rays the following day.

I spent three days in that hospital, and none of my relatives knew where I was. Shame prevented me from telling them. The shame that I knew my decision to play another season in that league had just cost me my dream!

When I was released from the hospital, my agent came to visit me. He walked in and expressed his disappointment, his anger. And on his way out the door, he said, "Well, it was a long shot anyway!"

I had time to think about it, and I asked myself a serious question: *How in the world could I have let this happen to me? I could have made history as the first Black punter in the NFL.*

Epilogue: Inspiration

I hope my experience, both the victories and the setbacks, can serve as inspiration for up-and-coming players and those in a position to coach and hire them.

To Aspiring Punters and Kickers

I would like to tell aspiring Black kickers at whatever level you're playing, if it's your dream or aspiration to reach the pinnacle of your position as kicker or punter, by all means necessary, pursue it.

Get the best coaching or teaching, and be true to it. Be true to your art, practice, build strength, and experiment with kicks, placements on foot, and drop heights in order to become the best by understanding how the ball reacts to what you're doing.

It's your dream—don't give it away at any cost! And believe me, you will get an opportunity someday. It's only a matter of time.

To Youth Leagues; High School, College And University Coaches; NFL Coaches, General Managers, Owners, And The NFL Commissioner

I know that things are changing all the time, yet it's still too slow. Black quarterbacks have shown their talents and are getting opportunities on the field. They are being watched from high school and recruited from the college level, and pro teams are benefiting from their talents.

The same should be true for Black kickers and punters. There have been fewer than ten Black men playing those positions in the pros in the last fifty years.

Come on, man! That's not change—that's continued screening. Those players are out there and they're good, waiting for a chance to be seen. So please, NFL, open your eyes and your hearts and I guarantee you, just as with the quarterbacks, you won't be disappointed and your teams will be made better!

Some years ago, there was a TV special featuring two Black kickers at the same college, one a punter, the other a placekicker.

Both had the same dream of being a Black kicker in the NFL. They were both aware of the fact that there had only been five positions filled by Blacks as kickers. Two or three of them were not even American-born Blacks, and all were former soccer players, a trend that was becoming more and more popular in the NFL. The majority of non-Black kickers in the league were conventional kickers at that time.

The league should understand that there are colleges that produce great Black punters and kickers who have or not played soccer. They deserve much more than just a looking at. They need to be seen as serious prospects and given an opportunity to show that they have what it takes to make it in professional football.

Acknowledgments

I thank God, my Heavenly Father, who gave me the athletic gifts, mindset, skills, and abilities, that I had the opportunity to reach a platform of such heights, namely the NFL tryouts.

I want to also thank my amazing wife, Marilyn. I am continually and eternally grateful for the depth of your commitment to the projects and journey God has laid out for us. Thank you for understanding the importance of my work in the Kingdom of God and humanity. Thank you for continuously interceding in prayer for me on what I am called by God to do. Thank you so much, sweetheart.

Special thanks to Marinna Castilleja, Kirkus Senior Production Editor for *4th And A Longshot*, along with the entire Kirkus Book Prep team, all of whom put in so much time, effort, and dedication to ensure this book was professionally edited, formatted, and book cover designed.

Special thanks to the entire BlesScott team on this *4th And A Longshot* book project. Thank you for your commitment as I share my football journey through writing. I am so blessed to have each of you as such a powerful support team, and your football experience and knowledge really brought excitement to the project; thank you all for volunteering your assistance.

About the Author

Nathan Scott had his first NFL kicking tryout at a Dallas Cowboys camp as a high school senior and was in the final tryout phase. Years later he had his second tryout with the Dallas Cowboys and a tryout with the Houston Oilers.

As a semi-pro football player, playing in the United Independent Football League (UIFL), Nathan received several awards: All-Pro safety second team, All-Pro kicker first team, and best safety strong side—first team.

As a sophomore kicker in high school, Nathan was named to the all-city and all-area teams (first team punter).

In April 2023, Nathan released an end-time novel, *WOE 1*, based on true events written about in the book of Revelation of the Holy Bible, which will come to pass in the future.

His professional career includes more than twenty-five years of experience in the aviation industry where he is currently employed. He lives with his wife, Marilyn, in Texas.